Sailing to Omeath

for the Goddess

Francis O'Hare

Sailing to Omeath

Sailing to Omeath

is published in 2020 by
ARLEN HOUSE
42 Grange Abbey Road
Baldoyle, Dublin 13, Ireland
Phone: 00 353 86 8360236
arlenhouse@gmail.com
arlenhouse.blogspot.com

978–1–85132–218–3, paperback

Distributed internationally by
SYRACUSE UNIVERSITY PRESS
621 Skytop Road, Suite 110
Syracuse, NY 13244–5290
Phone: 315–443–5534
Fax: 315–443–5545
supress@syr.edu
syracuseuniversitypress.syr.edu

Typesetting by Arlen House

Cover photo courtesy of the Mulligan family, Omeath

LOTTERY FUNDED

Contents

Sailing to Omeath

Sailing to Omeath

These images that yet
Fresh images beget.
– 'Byzantium', W.B. Yeats

Mulligan's Corner House
in Omeath, in the 1970s,
was my first ever glimpse of the marvellous,
an emperor's emerald palace
gilt by the evening sea's

glittering brine-holy haze.
Its sea-shelled window displays
and Byzantine dark passageways
held Waterford Crystal ablaze
in the sun's butterscotch glaze,

bedazzling as an oasis
a-shimmer with incense and spices
in the summery heat of sea breezes
blowing my mind, like young Keats',
as I stood, nose to glass, just to gaze

on genuine blackthorn shillelaghs,
fine Belleek china vases
ivied with shamrocks and roses,
prints of Dundalk in the twenties,
dolls in a cellophane gauze,

dream-woven tapestries
of legendary Gaelic heroes;
Cú Chulainn, Oisín, Deirdre's
flights and fights, ancient sorrows,
the Proclamation by Pearse

from the steps of the General Post Office
and, for me, the deep mysteries

of elaborately-hammered toys;
Hornby model railways,
one-thousand-piece dolphin-torn jigsaws,

sailing ships full-rigged to rise
above all mere complexities
my child mind imagined; the furies
of soldiers and blood back in Newry's
war-haunted streets, the atrocities

that nightly sang out from our telly's
grainy bad weather, the IRA's
latest bomb blast, burnt-out buses
in Belfast or Derry, some UDA
victim found dead in a back alley's

dawn-cold exposure … and above these
visions of half-earthly paradise,
there breathed, up on high, starlit statues
of the Blessed Virgin and Jesus,
His blood-sodden heart offered to us,

His lapis lazuli eyes
gazing down from the cross
at me, amidst liquorice, old lace,
sticks of rock, King crisps, candyfloss,
seagulls' shrieks, piercing; miraculous

as a fabulous golden bird's cries
in a once-troubled emperor's reveries
of star-luscious skies, jewel lustrous,
or my traversing through galaxies
as a child in Omeath in the seventies

in Mulligan's Corner House.

The Island

The island of me
has a changeable climate;
one day it's sunny,
the next day it's wet.

The rain can persist
for week upon week,
a dolorous mist
stretching from peak

of highest mountain
to low valley floor,
draping grey muslin
to every shore

so that each passing
ship on the blue
ocean surrounding
my island sails through

to sunnier climes,
more temperate places,
in search of good times,
welcoming faces,

leaving my cliffs
cold and morose
pondering what ifs
in seagullicose

wind-haunted silence
until the next day
when the brightest of suns
lights up the bay.

The Six Million Dollar Kid

When I was seven or eight
I became the Bionic Man.
I remember my spaceflight failed,
rockets exploding, then

me falling back to earth
at a hundred miles an hour,
then nothing much for ages
before waking up, as a doctor

said, 'Gentlemen, we have
the technology to rebuild him.'
There were flashing lights and beeping.
I went into a dream.

Then suddenly I awoke.
Running on treadmills, lifting
weights like a superhero,
seeing, hearing, feeling

stronger, faster, *better*
than anyone else on the planet.
And they gave me my own theme music!
And a brilliant red tracksuit!

And this weird but class sound effect
for when I was being bionic;
Nnnnnrrrrrrrnnnnggggggghhhhhhh,
or something like that. Fantastic!

But the deal was I must use my powers
for good, and I did, mostly.
Although sometimes I just showed off.
In the playground. Jumping out of a tree.

Bali

I grew up during the hunger strike's last stand,
when the thought of going on holiday to Bali
was beyond belief. The year that Bobby Sands
died defying Thatcher's criminal policy
we watched the riots in West Belfast, Short Strand,
Ardoyne, Bogside, *everywhere*, on TV

and felt the simmering anger of the cells
where men lay dying in their own effluvia
and flies buzzed like those rumours someone else
was near the end. That summer the IRA
gained more support, as seen on gable walls,
than at any time since the days of de Valera

and Collins back in the Civil War.
The whole country was waiting to erupt
like Krakatoa. Every day, the violence
grew more explosive, *literally*. Time stopped
every time a newsflash hit the screens
with grim tidings; another place blown up

or victim shot or hunger striker dead ...
And every day my Da drove off to Belfast
in the works van; to the Falls, the Shankill Road,
or somewhere where each killing was the latest
in 'a series of tit-for-tat', the news reported,
as my mum blessed herself, sorting out our breakfast.

And *that* was the year my cousin Tommy took us
down to Butlin's, in Mosney, County Meath,
in his new Ford Escort for our summer holidays.
We set off one morning mid-July in seeth-
ing heat to drive from Newry down through various
small towns draped in black, bewailing death

as if the banshee world of childhood tales
had come to life again in a weird folkloric
odyssey through time and space, our vehicle's
rear suspension suffering shock after shock
on the southern roads' notorious potholes
and the engine overheating, until, carsick,

we arrived in Butlin's mythical paradise
in middle Ireland. Noon. Beneath the glare
of an equatorial sun directly above us,
its eyesight trained like an army helicopter
on anything that moved, we heard the news
that another one had died. I don't remember

much about the rest of that day except
us driving home through an utterly exotic
silence that transmogrified the climate
into something terrible, volcanic,
like you'd find on an island formerly full of parrot-
shriek, monkey-screech; suddenly stilled, strange, *seismic.*

1985

When I walked out
of Woolworth's on Hill Street
that school lunchtime,
my copy of Lloyd Cole's

Rattlesnakes in my hands,
I was only intent
on getting lost in Amsterdam
with my brand new friend,

a girl with perfect skin,
as guitars chimed sweetly
in the never-ending blue
of adolescent afternoons

starting forest fires
in imagined hotel rooms,
reading Simone de Beauvoir
and kissing in the rain.

Little did I know
that not all those jingly-jangly
songs were as optimistic
as their melodies implied.

I should have waited, really,
a half lifetime or so,
or even read the lyrics
or listened to his voice,

and I might have saved
myself a lot of trouble,
mightn't have been so badly
heartbroken, suffered love bites.

April

I stood at the Stone Bridge with Joan McClean
amidst the April blossom, after school,
and talked of the future as afternoon sunshine
dappled the water below us, flowing, cool

and calm, through Newry towards the open sea,
past Warrenpoint, Omeath and Carlingford,
embracing pure blue possibility
as it entered the restless, wandering, wider world

our talk imagined. She was bound for London
at the start of the summer, after her exams,
while I was … I was … keeping my options open.
Maybe I'd head for Paris … or New Orleans …

Although I knew the only travelling I'd be
doing was in my head, or thumbing lifts
into or back home from Newry Library
all through the heat of July and August, drift-

ing through my daydreams till September
when I'd register to start my course at Queen's.
Meanwhile, Joan would work in a shop in Mayfair
and spend her nights in Piccadilly, scenes

of wild-child romance under London skies
being chatted up by French, Italian, Spanish
boys on mopeds, all dark hair and deep eyes
and skin as golden as their futures' promise.

Back on the bridge we stood in awkward silence
as her bus pulled up in the confetti disarray
of fallen blossom. I watched, with an awful sense
of fate, her take her seat and float away

into early evening traffic, as the first
spits of a sudden spring shower hit the surface
of the river flowing onward, fit to burst,
realising we'd forgotten our farewell kiss.

Yeah Yeah Yeah!

for Michael Sands

Friday nights, Drumalane,
in the top attic room
of your family's old house
we'd turn on, drink wine
or beer, the *Red Album*,
unutterably *fab*ulous,

on constant revolve
as we listened in wonder
to each song arise
like a rainbow or dove,
clean out of nowhere,
amidst our oasis.

How do they do it?
I used to exclaim
as another explosion
of noise left us winded,
filled up to the brim
and above with sheer passion

to conquer the world,
or, at least, Friday night
in Newry; our Guinness-
and-Beatles-songs-fuelled
marches by starlight
to a pub, where our genius

for failing with girls,
annoying some 'Ra-man,
would see us escaping
like pop stars, in swirls
of photo-lens action
up cobbled streets, dripping

with rain and romance;
those self-same stone cobbles
that four boys in suits
in Liverpool once
ran down, their boot heels
tapping wild backbeats.

And then we'd get back
to your house in the small hours,
dial down the roar,
have *more* drink, food, music
and crawl up the stairs,
you to bed, me the floor,

and drift into dreamland,
like Alice, our heads
swaying like sunflowers
to the sound of the band
spin golden threads
across Newry, the universe.

A Good Day to Die

for my Father

You died that day in the August rain,
killed by the shock of ten thousand volts,
not far from home, in Castlewellan,
putting in roadside electric lampposts,

after working in Belfast for twenty-odd years
and seeing the Troubles, in all their dirty-
war glory. Extortion gangs. Wee words in ears.
Death threats. Brown envelopes. Ireland free.

Or God and Ulster. Depending which week
the visit occurred. All divvied up fair
and square by the lads. It made you sick
watching them across the street on the corner

doing good business. Making good money
while you worked like a dog for barely a wage
worth all this grief, Monday to Saturday,
and sometimes Sunday, all through their 'rage

for order', disorder, a new order, whatever.
'Whoever wins', you said, 'it won't be us.
The ordinary fucker will stay fucked forever.'
A relief when your firm got the job to replace

the street lighting network outside the city.
You told my mum she'd not have to worry,
now that the work was out in the country,
handy and safe. Who knew what irony

meant back then? Maybe you learned
as you lay by the road in the rod-like rain,
whispering, 'Mary', your nerve-endings burned
black to the root, beyond mortal pain,

and life slipped away like flowing rainwater
downhill into a storm drain, to join
underground darkness, death, the hereafter –
whatever the word is. The war carried on.

SOMEDAY

you will leave your dank adolescence
in that small grey town full of nothing but rain
on a glorious morning at the end of September,
full of sunlight and birdsong, to step onto a train
glinting out of the distance, gleaming into the future,

where a city awaits like a signed early volume
of Yeats or Rimbaud, Baudelaire, Hart Crane,
or a rare LP, *The Freewheelin' Bob Dylan,*
uncertain of everything except your desire
to walk strange streets in search of experience,

that dazzling instant of nuclear renaissance
young Icarus felt in the sun's silent gaze
you dreamed of whilst lost in a Joycean fire.
There will be times, of course, when you stare
at the mildewed walls of your lonely room

but there'll come an epiphany, later that autumn,
over coffee in a secondhand bookshop,
when the world outside is all incandescence
with wonder and magic, leaf-shadowed by gloom,
like the faded front cover of your sacred album,

when you will encounter one whose wild essence,
like autumn sunshine, as she slowly looks up
to answer your question, will suddenly blaze
out of her dark eyes and you will remember,
during rainfall, this moment, on other dank days.

‘I Did Wonder …’

for Diarmuid Cromie

Remember us that August morning
nearly thirty years ago,
the sun already high and burning
in the blue air, clouds moving slow-
ly through the summer sky
like cattle on some western prairie?

On the road, to Belfast, thumbing
lifts from traffic, like our heroes,
Kerouac and Dylan, bumming,
Dharma-style, a pair of hobos,
bound for glory like Woody Guthrie
and hungry for the future, Newry

fading in the dusty distance
like some old sepia photograph
of a midwest town, a lonely train’s
whistle like a dead man’s laugh,
our farewell message of goodbye,
fixin’, as we were, to die

or die trying to make New York
or San Francisco – well, Belfast –
before the ancient highway broke
our youthful spirits or our last
cigarette got smoked, the empty
pack our will and testimony.

So, anyway, the sky was blue
and walking wasn’t suffering;
a friend to share the road with; you,
the high school football god, blithe morning
bright with birdsong bee-hum; me
the dreaming poet; suddenly

a car slows down on the A1's edge
and a door opens. We jump right in,
not taking time to think or hedge
our meagre bets, or even question
who's offering this charity.
This was God's hand. Destiny.

And that's the way it was. Our lift
turned out to be a man of God,
a minister and his wife, both soft-
ly spoken, sincere, kind-hearted,
asking about university,
recommending their church's chaplaincy

and generally passing the time until
the skyline of Belfast appeared
like Gotham City; huge, dark, still,
in the front windscreen. Were we scared?
Excited? Well, we smelt the sea,
heard the gulls, sensed that we

were entering a New Orleans
and maybe were a little nervous
about the prospect, the midday sun's
rising shadow ominous
as we drove into the glaring city
full of tension, hope, anxiety

leaping up like buildings, tall
and full of windows ... then, remember,
the wife's last words that said it all,
down by the docks, 'I did wonder ...'
as we thanked them for their help, the high
cranes like statues, things of beauty.

Belfast Gothic

It has to be The Cure and *Disintegration*,
in a room in the Holy Lands, at the end of the 80s
or the start of the 90s, pure alienation
bleeding out of their most mournful of LPs

as we sit in near darkness, except for a few
candles burnt down to their flickering stumps,
at the ends of our wits, just me and you
and the spidery shadows and the jolts and the jumps

of the needle running in endless, sad circles
through the grooves of the record, like us through the reasons
you couldn't love me, or like Dante through Hell's
spiralling vortex ... outside, the seasons

drift through themselves in a drugged semi-trance;
autumn, spring, summer, winter – then more
autumn again as the leaves do that dance
of twirling around in the twilight forever

all true Cure fans know in their bones, and the street
fades to grey, dawn emerging out of the dark
like Robert Smith rising up from his winding sheet
and climbing in through the window-frost's lacework ...

A Street

It was an early morning street, its quiet distances still small secrets shared by night with day.
– At Swim-Two-Birds, Flann O'Brien

Everything was sacred
in the 7am
incense, your aftertaste
wine-sharp on my tongue

after our very first
encounter, the taxi ride,
sitting up, talking, kissing,
till, suddenly, aware

of darkness's declension
into grey dapple,
mid-October leaflight,
feather delicate

chamber group acoustics
of birdsong trellising
your garden, dew-original
glimpses of green hills

emerging out of silence,
suburbia withholding
approval, not unkind,
dawn blessed, I'd slipped

out into the coolness
and otherness of morning,
lightheaded, in love,
christened by existence,

to stand, overwhelmed,
in the whole shimmering

Indian-summery city's
rose-rich largesse,

its rivers, swallow-paths,
wood-flowers, sea-aromas,
sense-memories, footsteps
echoing themselves

in the early morning
street, its quiet distances
still small secrets shared
by day with night.

Astral Weeks

A sweetheart from another life floats there
– 'An Image from a Past Life', W.B. Yeats

As long as this music exists
I'll be twenty-two and wandering through
a cherry-blossomed avenue
in leafy-with-love-that-loves-to-love Belfast,

an impromptu symphony
of starlings and skylarks constantly singing
soul-paeans to the sunshine, church bells ringing
out in epiphany

the sweet, sweet, summer-
time of the past,
until out of sea-myst-
ical evening, mysteriously, you shimmer,

vision-like, sauntering, your perfume drifting
through my mind like guitars,
the first silent stars
in sapphire skies glistening, heavenly, listening

to the wind and the rain in my soul, sense-transcendent
of, ballerina-like, pain,
to breathe in your hair, to be born again,
my arm round your waist in that pure instant

in the lilac and blue
wonder of being, in cool night air,
and we forget who we were
before we were here, wet with raindrops and dew,

in the eternal *now,*
cherry blossoms falling weaving arabesques of feeling

as we stand at a railing,
a train blowing out its harmonica solo,

and then we'll have kissed
as we watch the moon shine
above Shalimar, feeling almost divine
as long as this music exists.

That Morning

for Ursula

Your skin, soft, cold as September,
awoke my hunger for kisses.
Outside, the street blushed, self aware,
conscious of sunlight, appearances.

Our room, two floors up, was a submarine
grotto of perfumed sea breezes
blowing in, caressing the curtain,
casting mist on the mirror's distances.

Sycamore trees cast diaphanous
leaf-lacy silk on your shoulder,
and, gracing your throat, a necklace
of shadow-light, violet-veined, smouldered.

The cool of that morning, like linen,
lingered in limbs pure as lilies
as bedsheets, impatient as children,
slipped floorward, breath held, naughtily.

And then your body was naked
as autumn and I was your lover
touching, like sunshine or seaweed,
your lips, your breasts, ever lower,

your skin, soft, cold as September,
kissing love into your veins
until, sighing slow as a river,
you opened your eyes, and it rained.

Lovebirds

Once we were lovebirds. We lived on a wing
and a prayer. You were pretty. I was learning to sing
your lips' cloudy magic, rosebud-red, opening
to kiss me, console me, heal everything.

Nothing could hurt us as we flew through the air
cartwheeling, *free*wheeling, with 'nary a care',
not seeing the future loom, unaware
of the wall of indifference the world likes to prepare

for dreamers like us in love with cheap flight
above houses, dull jobs, the dismal foresight
of sensible doom-merchants, assured they were right
when they happily sermoned against chasing the light

and told us to come back down to earth,
get a grip on ourselves, and value the worth
of not walking on air but solid ground; mirth-
less, respectable, real, sober as death,

but we laughed at their wisdom and continued to float
through our lives like the scarves round a wild dancer's throat
until one day you told me, your lips pursed, you owed it
to yourself to come out of the clouds, grabbed your coat,

as the sky crashed into me. Huge. Hard hearted.
A city of strangers. A mountain of granite.
Smashing my wings as if they were cardboard.
Sending me hurtling, heartbroken, earthward.

Her Perfume

Postmodern existence flies
at a thousand miles-per-hour.
I prefer to walk,
smell the occasional flower.

A girlfriend I once had
would *run* up escalators
while I stood still, awaiting
the best possible of futures,

her standing at the top,
tutting impatiently.
She couldn't appreciate
the vision I *still* see

of her there, a blown rose,
proud, in all her prime,
full-throated, firm, immortal,
transcending wasteful time,

but the world demands we rush
and we split soon afterwards.
We haven't kept in touch.
Her perfume wrote these words.

Last Night of the Twentieth Century

New Year's Eve … Merlot ... the full-bodied scent
of frost-fragrant streets, star-blossomed skies,
smoky bars in the city, ruby lips, charcoaled eyes,
soul music in cellars, the astral estrangement

wrought by the moon, and a crystalline fire
to encounter again the witchcraft of women
through alcohol-mists; wine-dark subterranean-
shadowy sirens, waterfalls of desire …

I was sitting alone, listening to Cohen
strumming guitar in a broken lament,
Marlborough-moaning memories of ancient
heartbroken evening, where a glorious green

sunset silhouetted two beautiful losers
on a Venetian gondola. They were talking of love
as if they were the only two people alive
and the world a dustheap of embers, lost empires.

The Mediterranean moonlight brought glamour
to the woman's dark eyes, the man's moving lips,
his eternal sighs over her hips
salting the twilight like a sea-born zephyr,

but what they were saying in this tragic opera,
this doomed romance under cold stars
casting diamonds in midnight-still waters,
deep as the heart of queen Cleopatra,

was lost in the mist that rolled over me
as I drifted to sleep on that river of sound,
to dream of one woman, in a sleep so profound
I lost myself in its music, enwound as a mummy

who once looked on all as a lord or a king,
who looked now on life through the mirror of death
from his own ghostly element, fine as wine breath,
and woke a thousand years older next morning.

Twenty Autumns

Twenty autumns since I loved you
Twenty autumns of falling leaves
Twenty autumns of desolation
Twenty autumns of wind that sieves

Twenty autumns of listening to Cure songs
Twenty autumns of talking to walls
Twenty autumns of annihilation
Twenty autumns of empty wine bottles

Twenty autumns of pointless Wednesdays
Twenty autumns of rainy streets
Twenty autumns of desperation
Twenty autumns of bloodstained sheets

Twenty autumns of waking nightmares
Twenty autumns of eating beans
Twenty autumns of alienation
Twenty autumns of ugly scenes

Twenty autumns of Pablo Neruda
Twenty autumns of *nil desperandum*
Twenty autumns of isolation
Twenty autumns of bottomless autumn

Second Glance at the Muse

O what can ail thee knight-at-arms,
Alone and palely loitering?
The sedge has withered from the lake,
And no birds sing!
– 'La belle dame sans merci', John Keats

Her tarot darkness
pervades my mind
like swirling marsh gas;
stumbling, blind,

I flounder through
a gothic landscape,
storm-lit, blue,
of moorland, clifftop

above a sea
as black as night
that mouths at me
with foaming white

fangs of hunger,
ravenous,
as I stagger
on, my face

lashed by branches
of the wind,
blood-streaked, anxious,
towards a ruined

mansion glowering
in the moon's
gloom-glow, towering
over, runes

carved on the door;
Abandon hope,
All ye who enter,
through which I grope

to find myself,
as in a dream,
before a sylph-
like vampire queen,

her eyes aflame
but cold and dead
as lithium
inside my head

and suddenly
I know I've come
to what will be
my mausoleum.

SEPTEMBER

Once,
on Eglantine,
I strolled
through April sunshine

and saw
the green-tongued leaves
bursting
out of trees,

feeling
supersonic,
original,
bionic,

but these
September days,
though still
a shimmer-haze,

are different;
in my forties
I feel
the autumn breeze.

47

Having reached the age
of the Steppenwolf
I turned the page
to discover myself

living alone
in a fog-entombed city,
a wounded faun
among the bourgeoisie,

alone with the bottle,
my music, my books,
through a season in hell,
lycanthropic attacks

of animal lust,
taverns and women,
days and nights lost
in lupine oblivion,

my only escape
from this bottomless nightmare
at the end of a rope
or the edge of a razor,

until, hallow-eyed, gaunt,
I walked through morning
in love with the quaint
ornateness of birdsong

in search of that true
love that the poets
write of (that *you*
who inspires cosmic sonnets)

to appear in the haze
of narcotic dawn
and with just one kiss
on the lips lead me on

to a magical show
down a hallway of doors,
each one of them o-
pening onto a universe.

Grief

Somewhere not too far from where we are
there's a place beyond the pale of all belief.
It can't be reached by telephone or car.
Google Maps won't help you. To be brief,
it's not quite of this world and yet, however,
it does exist. It has a name. It's Grief.

In the town of Grief the people all wear black
and greet each other with 'Sorry for your troubles'.
It's always November and always four o'clock,
the cold air bleak with constant screams of gulls,
for the town of Grief is near the sea, its wrack
pervasive as the smell of death, of funerals.

The streets are always empty for no one goes
about their daily business, due to 'sad
unforeseen events', though each one knows
that such events are all foreseen and fated
or else they wouldn't be in this lachrymose
place where even sunlight is grey and faded.

In all the dark three-storey-tall townhouses
blinds are pulled and oil lamps dimly burn
in shadowed parlours, full of doleful faces
and longeurs stretching into endless mourn-
ful silence over curling sandwiches
and dregs of tea like ashes in an urn.

And always, in a top room, by themselves,
sit white-dressed ones who can't accept that this
is how they must see out their lonely lives,
transfixed and rapt by Mozart's Requiem Mass
and wondering over all the dull what ifs
that led them up these stairs, to this strange solace.

Reading Nadezhda Late at Night

I have studied the science of separations,
Night's sorrows, when a woman's hair falls down.
– 'Tristia', Osip Mandelstam

Reading the memoir by his widow,
I heard the ticking of a clock
and, further off, the sound of snow
falling was a seismic shock.

I heard the ancient river, time,
roaring through me as I read
and understood why Mandelstam
wrote his poetry in blood.

He had to sing what he had heard
in all its crystal haeccitas
before 'the age' shoved him aboard
a cattle train for outer space,

or Vladivostok – who can tell
where poets go who dare to hear
(a transit camp or Dante's Hell)
night's sorrows in some fallen hair?

CARLINGFORD

I will arise and go now, and go to Carlingford,
and a small B&B room rent there, with en-suite bathroom
    supplied:
Nine oysters will I have there, and a glass of wine afterward,
and sleep alone in the hen-loud night.

And I shall read some Yeats there, for Yeats feels like the rain,
falling in the early morning to where the alarm call rings.
There midnight's all a downpour, and noon a pint of plain,
and evening full of the seagull's wings.

I will arise and go now, for as I drive to work each day,
I hear sea water slapping with slow sounds in my ear.
While I sit at a zebra crossing, or on the motorway,
I hear it, more urgent every year.

Hilltown

I: Midweek

In Hilltown it's a Hilltown sort of evening.
The mountains are a postcard-perfect backdrop,
all misty-Mourneful in the drizzle-distance,
to not much happening. The village's one street
is quiet tonight, like most nights during the week.
There's a few odd punters in the Downshire Arms,
couples mainly, one old guy at the bar
finishing his pint, and down the street
the Shamrock pub has football on the telly;
a midweek repeat of *The Sunday Game*, half-watched
by the only barman, killing time to closing
and his stroll home via the chip shop, under stars
peeping their heads out through the fraying clouds
and wondering who is out and about this late.

II: The Weekend

In Hilltown it's a Hilltown sort of evening.
The INF hall is full of girls in croptops
and boys outside drinking out of Harp cans
in rolled-up sleeves despite the rain-cum-sleet
that's rolling off the mountains. Hilltown chic
demands no less than spray tans, muscled arms
on show at all times no matter what the weather.
The older punters know the score and meet
in warmer climates, fire-lit, preferably,
and re-enact last Sunday's football match
against the 'Bridge, or take their time in choosing
a new manager for Down … in all the bars
wives and girlfriends are sipping vodkas, Pernods,
and wondering what brought them to this fate.

OMEATH

In Warrenpoint, as kids, we'd gaze out over
the grey and grisly, seagull-squally Lough,
past coal boats churning into the old harbour,
to see Omeath, resplendent, gazing back
at us across the bay, a sunlit daughter
of celandine and fuchsia, always beck-
oning us to sail out, cross the water
into the clear blue skies of the Republic
and leave behind our grimy, humdrum Ulster
seaside town for something more exotic;
a paradise of pampas, palm trees, sapphire
twilights we imagined were half-magic,
until the rain came on and it was time for
home, the lost horizon tear-struck, tragic.

A Field in Mid-Summer

Somewhere between Dundalk and Castleblaney
there's a field of corn the colour of nostalgia.
I found it once, in the middle of July,
on one of those days you wish you had a camera
but don't, so all you can do is park the car
and dander through a golden landscape, dreaming
of Francis Ledwidge, that summer before the War,
musing on butterflies, transience and women,

the heat of history beating on his back
as he walked a field like this one last sweet time,
the buzz and drone of bees, the dull *ack ack*
of a corncrake somewhere, heartbreaking as rhyme
offered to a girl whose heart is cold
as earth is in the black-iced depths of winter
in no man's land, the fragrance of an old
sorrow haunting his memory of her

as he held his hands out to touch the living day,
the spider-peopled silence of a field
in the central plain of Ireland, filled with fey
glimmerings of poppy flowers that yield-
ed something of a sense of his own path
through torn-up cornfields later on in France,
the golden days of youth and love blown south
like roses, lips, poems, summer's essence.

Dandelion Heads

for my aunt Brigid McCann

I watched you die as summer drifted
through cloudless days, like dandelion
heads through high-grassed fields. Between
the home and hospital you shuttled.
Towards the end, though, morphine let you
stray through your own childhood, picking

flowers in the back fields in Crobane
to bring in to your mother, brightening
the Sunday teatime parlour, all kinds
of everything; buttercups, bluebells, foxgloves,
violets, daffodils, roses, primroses,
daisies, and even the odd dandelion

granted its few brief hours in the sun
of Sunday evening, before your father
would dim the light in the two oil lamps
illuminating the delft in the dresser,
the mahogany table, china, silver,
of that burnished room, leaving you all,

you, your brothers and sisters, my granny,
in fading twilight at the end of July,
with no option but bed, your prayers, and sleep
in the gossamer silence, perchance to dream
of floating over a summery field, like
seed clouds, blown, wished upon, airborne.

A Hero's Funeral

I was stuck in rush-hour congestion
trying to get home from work,
surfing the dial over stations
when news of his sudden death broke
like a tidal wave over that Friday,
washing away the next week,
till I landed up in Bellaghy
graveyard, unable to speak,
but hearing September's rich music
of birdsong in trees and the air
alive with a piper's sweet homesick
lamentings and yearnings, aware
of a deeper bass note, the rare silence
left when heroes sail over horizons.

Field Worker

i.m. Seamus Heaney

It makes sense
to stand at a gate
and contemplate
experience,

to gaze out over
an empty hay field
in early September,
its ample yield

being baled and stooked
and grown golden
as bannock, baked
under the sun,

now home and dry
in an outhouse somewhere
safe until winter
founders the sky

and hungry bastes
come back to byres
for a precious taste
of summer pastures.

It fills you up
with gratefulness
to linger thus
and take your sup

of the dying day,
having earned your rest,
having worked the hay,
brought in the harvest.

TIMETABLES
for JH

Our school timetabler's
tone is light,
but I sense the sigh;

'Those self-same stars
I watched last night
compose the sky

have seen all wars
and empires; bright,
saw Jesus die.'

Homebird

for my aunt Brigid O'Hare

July 1970,
mini-skirted, a beehive;
that's you cradling me
in my first photograph.

After that, I can
hardly ever remember
you not in an apron.
Year after year,

on Sunday visits,
while Frances and Sheila
would take us on walks
up the back fields,

picking blackberries,
seeing 'the well',
or just keeping an eye
on hay or cattle,

you were the home-
bird, flitting about the
wheaten and jam
in the wee back scullery,

a chaffinch, a wren,
a starling, a thrush,
a sparrow; 'say when ...',
'have ye's all had enough?'

You knew all the birds
that flew into the garden,
their names, all the words
of their songs, an adept in

all kinds of bird lore.
In winter, when redbreasts
came to the back door
you fed them crusts

and nattered to them
as if they were family.
When you left us, then,
and died suddenly,

it was just like a robin,
who has always been there,
in a wing-flash being gone
into thin air.

At Home with the Poet

In my Wildean parlour
I sit and take tea
with *The Phantom of the Opera*
and Salvador Dali

while, outside my window,
Neruda's dream land
of kisses, volcanoes,
rises out of the sand

of this dull Belfast street's
lone, level landscape
like the phantasmal figures
Dali sees in his teacup

or the heavenly music
the Phantom can hear
in the way the clock ticks,
the sigh of the fire,

until late afternoon
fills the room with new guests;
centaurs, satyrs and fauns,
and the faces of ghosts

who stare from my mirrors
and blank TV screen
in a mute twilit chorus;
shadow-dark, green

with envy for those lives
they never quite led
beyond enchanted forests,
sacred groves of the dead.

Street Music

O cold, wet streets of Newry
on a rainy Friday night
glistening with mystery,
under streetlamps, starlight,
your names compose a litany,
a prayer, a lonely flight

beyond the valley vapour,
chip shop, taxi rank,
nightclub, pub, river,
canal, cathedral, bank,
town hall, courthouse, Ulster-
bus station, dank

small-town air pervading
my soul like John Coltrane
on *Spiritual*, the tinkling
jazz piano strain
gently harmonising
with horn, like wind and rain

that blows and falls through all
these streets, this town, this me –
alert, observant, neutral,
aware of history
and Wallace Stevens' angel
of necessity; poetry

in tune with what is here;
lovers' late night rows,
shouts for taxis, laughter
spilling out of shadows
like rain from a shopfront gutter
around midnight ... now's

the time for me to listen,
in this almost-silence,
to the sound of falling rain
on wet streets, its soft opulence
a rich drip-drop refrain
heard after the last note ends:

River, Quay, Canal,
Mary, Mill, O'Hagan,
Dominic, Talbot, Castle,
Baggot, Barrack, Catherine,
Chapel, Church, John Mitchell,
Kiln, Kildare, Monaghan …

Memento

Picture this;
a young woman,
her back to us,
in sleety rain,

above her, sky
Soviet-grey,
a seagull's cry
not far away,

a cold air which
reminds us of
Shostakovich's
The Second Waltz,

and swirls us back
to Leningrad,
that paranoiac
world frost-clad,

but she is music;
is violins,
is clarinets
and saxophones,

her body light
as a melody,
or a dove in flight
above the sea.

She wears a hood
against the weather
so what her mood
is, we never gather

until she turns
(remember this)
on us. And burns
like ice. Like roses.

Meeting the Goddess

These winter mornings, driving through
the darkness down back country roads
I find myself attentive to
the moon, in all her moods and modes.

One minute she is Cleopatra,
solemn in her tragic mask,
the next, a 1920s flapper;
Louise Brooks, dark eyes askance.

And then she disappears from sight
as trees or clouds obscure my vision,
like some Victorian *Woman in White*,
elusive as an apparition

until I turn a sudden corner
and drive into another world
where everything is monochrome – a
spectral landscape, strange and cold,

uncanny as surrealist paintings
composed of clocks and marble nudes,
or Neolithic stone engravings
full of indecipherable runes,

where only moon law operates;
ancient, distant, pitiless …
a realm that both exhilarates
and terrifies; home of the goddess.

Isis at the Christmas Do

The usual forced festive yuletide scene
of Staff Welfare day. Beauty and Health
are both on the menu. A hit with the women,
jiving and having the time of their lives
in a glitter-ball haze: *Dancing Queen …*

After a term trying to teach Shakespeare's
dream of proud Mark Antony's fall
my mind is astray on far Alexandria's
lass unparalleled, all dull sense dispelled,
when she enters, enchanting my gaze

until our great general's words, *Let Rome*
in Tiber melt, and the wide arch
of the ranged empire … suddenly come
to my own lips, watching (her swaying hips,
her dress – sea and fire, just like Actium!)

Thus, though I feign pure nonchalance,
how can I hold this unearthly young woman
in the civilised imposture of dance
when all I desire is to kiss her and lose
myself in her dark hair's romance?

And all the while, as I pretend unconcern,
how can I sit at this restaurant table
and sip the white wine of decorum
when she sits across from me, crossing her legs,
capsizing my calm, like a siren?

For, despite the best of my Roman efforts,
I can't stand, at this Christmas drinks party,
to trade meaningless 'banter' with colleagues
whilst she floats through the room, like some Eastern
perfume, or Queen Cleopatra, that goddess!

The Morning After

for Adrian & Una

As I sit here listening, this Christmas Eve,
to an early tape of the young Bob Dylan
playing Woody Guthrie songs in what, I believe,
is his first recorded reincarnation
as a railway-hobo-bluesman-cum-poet,
I think of a year ago, travelling home
the morning after I'd crashed on your sofa bed,
broken-hearted, friendless, drunken and lonesome
as a dustbowl loser in the mid-1930s,
and watching those train stations, mile after mile,
and thanking the Lord for mornings like these
and friends like you two, and starting to smile
as the sky above me started to brighten
and the load on my shoulders started to lighten.

Wonder

It seems like only a sleigh bell's shake
since this time last year, but the first snowflake
of winter touched my face today
and, snowflake-like, I was carried away
to a Christmas morning decades ago,
trudging to mass through light, falling snow,
and seeing the world, for the very first time,
as wonderful, strange, perfected, like rhyme;
a crystalline silence purifying the air,
all around me the countryside forming a choir
of birdsong and cattle waking up to the wonder
of the Kingdom of God, born again, under
a County Down sky, still sleepy with stars,
as I held my da's hand, in this wide universe.

SNOWPRINTS

A poem is footsteps through snow –
a completely original sign
of something; who, or *what*, we don't know
but guessing is fun ... to define

its significance further than that
is simply impossible. Listen;
the silence of snow is articulate
of nothing. But listen again

to the whiteness of this blank page
as you walk in it, hearing each step
you take slowly utter a language
unheard before, foreign, its depth

as expressive as birdsong, as fresh
as meltwater trickling down through
tree branches above, a pure mesh
of sound-music, making you new

as you arrive at the edge of yourself
and, looking back, find that you've led
yourself by the hand through a forest
of meaning, your path neatly printed.

The Sixth of January

for Paul and John Devlin

We drive through the bleak post-Christmas drizzle
of January sales crowds, through Newry, Dundalk
and on to Blackrock. A dull sky says all
that needs to be said. We get out and walk

along the seafront, silent, *sans* seagull,
lacking the spirit for epiphany, small talk.
Three not-so-wise wiseguys out for a stroll
on a cold afternoon in mid-winter. A Prufrock-

ian frost-fog. Drab glitter and tinsel
decorating shop windows. The sun's made of chalk.
A pint would help celebrate the season of goodwill
but the pubs all seem to be under padlock.

A lane off the main street invites our perusal;
a derelict house with painted-in flock-
curtains is chilling as a Stephen King novel
where you feel yourself watched by the absence you stalk,

and the growing suspicion that nothing is real
enters your mind like an axe in the back,
but we came here in search of *something*, spiritual
rebirth, maybe, or some souvenir rock –

the inns all closed, no sign of a stable,
almost a waste land, this ghostly republic,
so we climb the sad path to your old childhood chapel,
and gaze at the first evening stars. Four o'clock.

Rostrevor

The glitter-glory of winter sunlight, sea,
is the magic of this place; an epiphany.

Biographia Literaria

Somewhere between here
and the time of the prophets
I dated and married
the autumn wind.

We breezed through the pages
of *The New York Poets*
and honeymooned in
the Italian renaissance,

double dated with Shakespeare
and his Dark Lady,
dining by moonlight
and hydrogen brisance

as dolphins played madrigals
composed by the sea
that sang in our veins
while another day dawned.

Sometime around now
I questioned existence
with Jean Paul and Albert,
who spontaneously yawned

and left me alone
with my family portraits
in a room in Greenwich
Village, my destiny

written in blood
on the glass of a mirror
hung upside-down over
a glass of Madeira.

LISTEN

O the pathos
of old 45s,
those ghostly voices
haunting their grooves:

Elvis Presley
in Sun Studio,
'Blue Moon's' lonely
existentialist echo.

John Lennon's scream
on 'Twist and Shout'
sounding like pain
turned inside-out.

Marianne Faithfull,
in cracked monotone,
hymning 'The House
of the Rising Sun',

and early Dylan,
throat filled with dust
from riding a freight train
through the Midwest.

Lost in an attic,
or under the stairs,
the vinyl magic
of long lost eras,

I love those records,
their 'wild mercury sound'
charting the heart's
needle-scored wound.

Carpe Diem

Go on, lean in. Listen, you hear it? – Carpe – hear it? Carpe, carpe diem, seize the day, boys, make your lives extraordinary.
– Dead Poets Society

The class of today slump in their chairs,
assessing me with their Komsomol stares.
I take it for granted that they're only here
to get an exam pass; the notion of 'sheer
morning gladness', or 'the ripeness is all',
being sheer, bloody madness, lunatic drivel.

I watch them regard me with customers' eyes,
suspicious of beauty or truth – luxuries.
What they want, and will get, is standardised notes
on methods and context, 'significant' quotes
to put in their answers next May or June.
They all dream of A stars; never the moon.

I WON'T BE IN TODAY, BECAUSE …

I'm sick. There's something green and horrible
writhing inside me; a maggot-metropolis,
Dante's inferno, Troy about to fall,
Jesus receiving Judas's tainted kiss,
a Blakean rose, Dorian Gray's portrait,
early twentieth-century Dublin's paralysis,
Rimbaud's absinthe-visions, desolate
neon nights in New York City, tanks
rolling into Prague, the Soviet state,
the Manson family, post 9/11 Yanks
eyeing the world, Al Qaeda, Jews
in transit through Europe to concentration camps,
Syrian massacres, 24/7 news,
the horror of being with others, their fucking *views*!

Dear Editor

Let us in, mate. Don't be a cunt. Go on.
What's it to you if I've had a few – a *skinful*?
That's a bit much. I've seen me worse. I'm fine.
No need to act the big man, like a tool.
I promise, I'll just sit there, on my own,
away from the VIPs, the 'beautiful'
people posting their glamorous lives online
on *TwatsApp, Witter,* whatever ... your worst table
will do for me. That and a glass of wine
is all I ask. The place isn't even half full;
the same old lousy furniture, the brown
wallpaper that's been there since Finn Mac Cool,
the same sad fucks in the Last Chance Saloon.
Why am I even here? This joint's a hole!

Fine

What's it all about, I ask no one,
driving into work in pouring rain
through Ballymena's one-horse-it-died town
on another Monday morning, anodyne
with humdrum skies humped up to the horizon
and advertising hoardings for fake tan,
sofa sales and holidays in the sun.
It doesn't help when I turn the radio on
and they're playing 'Creep' by Radiohead, a drone
that's guaranteed to bring on deep depression
or *deeper*, I should rather say … but then
I notice something through my blurred windscreen;
a glimpse of whitethorn in a local garden
that glows cerise and, suddenly, it's *fine*!

A Daffodil

is a little yellow gramophone
playing *The Rite of Spring*
across the prison yard of winter.

And every shivering prisoner
who hears its sacred song
thanks his own Andy Dufresne.

The Cross

for Frank Sewell

I carried the cross of myself
through the demon-loud city,
suffered the thorns of their laugh-
ter, ridicule, anger and pity,
up the hill of Golgotha,
where they nailed me to a tree

and raised me up as a king,
anointed in my own blood.
I saw the temple falling
and finally understood
what it was I had been saying
to the sheep-like multitude

all these months and years.
I saw my mother below,
her face a veil of tears,
the woman with eyes of shadow,
a few drunken Roman soldiers
and I cried out, in wretched ego,

Aloi, why hast thou forsaken
me, up on this shameful cross?
And then it was that a vision
of freedom passed over my eyes
and I saw the heavens open,
found my salvation in loss.

Mary Magdalene's Vision

The stone was rolled away, the tomb left empty.
The darkness of the previous week had passed.
The land was filled with living light, which meant He
was *here, among* us, His true self, at last;
not some outcast, hung up on a cross,
but *love* itself, freed from mortal dross

and standing in the sunshine of the morning.
I'd come there in my bitter desolation.
Where else was there to go, filled with such mourning?
I thought the grave my only consolation
and now I'd found the stone was rolled away,
the tomb left empty, on this peaceful Sunday.

They'd called me 'whore' and 'harlot' in their Sanhedrin;
that temple made of stone, like their cold thought.
Moloch was their master; he and Mammon.
They never preached against being sold and bought
except when they weren't guaranteed their gold,
the profit lost when I witnessed the stone unrolled

and the tomb left empty, empty as the sky …
except it *wasn't* empty. Small birds flew
above the green earth, dispersing melancholy,
and through the green trees of the earth there blew
a cool, calm, revivifying wind
that calmed and cooled, refreshed my dried-up mind …

and then it was I saw Him, clothed in light.
He stood there, strange and terrible; yet kind
as lovers are … not judging, the Risen Christ,
asking me to leave the dead behind
and follow Him into His morning vision
of birdsong, greenness, opened tombs and sunshine.

EASTER, 2016

Belfast's *bling* in late March sunshine, sparkling
with early springtime's promise. Trees are glad-green
beneath blue skies. Streets are just *bedazzling*
after a shower of cherry-bud-ripening rain.

The man next door's been whistling all morning.
His wife's in bed still, enjoying days like these,
and as she wakes and stretches, smiling, yawning,
he's heading upstairs with a fry and a pot of Tetley's

and humming along to Van on Radio Ulster,
outside, starlings, blackbirds, swallows singing …
Wouldn't it be great if it were like this … they almost twitter,
winging the chorus, an ordinary beauty dawning

on shining roofs, domes, spires; born in the east,
reaching out over the Lough, the gantries, arching,
a wonderful rainbow above City Hall to the west
and the Black Mountain, glistening, like an *aisling*.

SWEET

Is there anything sweeter
than that brief moment
pulling out past a tractor
on a grassy-verged back road

on a sunny May morning,
the radio on;
'Me and Bobby McGee'
sung by Janis Joplin,

when you feel like a king
or a fleet-footed god
of this … *everything* –
the whole blooming world

of pinkness and mauveness
and greenness and blueness
and yellowness, whiteness –
this sheer shining bliss?

Well, maybe, that lift-
off over a humped-
back bridge, that so soft
stomach-dropped, goose-bumped

feeling of flying
like when you were there,
airborne, hardly breathing,
that one time, with *her*.

PERFECT

for Marese

In the evening light
of Magherafelt,
in a short dress so tight
and your body so svelte,
you beglamoured the night
like an actual starlet

crossing the sky
as you crossed the street
so elegantly
on your high-heeled feet
you sent my heart high-
er than heaven, my sweet,

and though there was rain
in the Magherafelt air
you were lit up with wine
and just didn't care
if it threatened to ruin
your glistening hair

as you danced in my brief
moment of vision
like a shimmering leaf,
or like Niamh tempting Oisín
to the land of lost youth,
or just like a woman

in the evening light
of Magherafelt
on a wet Friday night
except the perfume I smelt
in your wake was so right
I christened it *Perfect*.

Rain

May and though the skies *were* blue
it's raining now. What else is new?
But it's that soft romantic rain
you see in films, blurring pain
on an avenue, or a boulevard,
a grimy street, a grim backyard,
falling on the lonely lead-
ing man or woman, implying need
of that someone to walk through rain
with, in that Eden lovers gain
in single leaps, by eye contact:
you do? she weeps … The final act:
our lovers kiss, midst soaring strings
and sunlight, trees, birds' flutterings.

The Rain Again

When it comes to you I'm jealous of the rain,
that oh-so-smooth Lothario full of sighs,
touching you softly, breaking my heart again.

I know it's not cool, stylish or urbane
to feel this way, but I can't feel otherwise –
when it comes to you I'm jealous of the rain

kissing you on a street to an oboe's strain
transcending, Woody Allen-style, all worries,
touching you softly, breaking my heart again,

and whispering sweet nothings of its pain
when you're not there, to your ingénue's surprise.
When it comes to you I'm jealous of the rain;

it knows the strings to pluck your love to gain,
how to gaze into your darkened eyes.
Touching you softly, breaking my heart again,

it puts its arm around you in the wan-
ing lamplight, under starstruck skies.
Then it comes to me ... I'm jealous of *the rain*!
Touching you softly. Breaking my heart. Again.

A Spell

I wish it was a winter's night
and you and I were in our bed
in an old house in the glens, firelight
shadow-flickering overhead

from the turf fire in our bedroom hearth,
wind and rain outside at war
in branches of the trees, the earth
holding on to a single star

in the lonely blackness of the sky
for guidance through the stormy seas
of midnight's moment, your warm thigh
suggestive of love's mysteries.

I wish I had a wizard's spell
to alter laws of time and space.
I'd conjure us a magical
doorway from our separateness

and lead us through it to that room
where we would lie, by soft firelight,
and watch our ardour leap and loom
like spirits in the endless night.

A Bond

for lovers on their wedding day

We stand before the altar of our Lord
asking him to consecrate our love.
Around us: loved ones, family, friends, are 'gathered
here today to witness', as we give
in offering, as sacrifice, ourselves;
our freedom as free agents, to be joined
in holy marriage, out of which evolves
our new selves; reborn, alchemised, fresh-coined.
In giving you my hand and taking yours
we forge a symbol of our deepest trust
in something that is unseen, yet endures;
a bond that cannot shatter, warp or rust,
a bond that is made golden in these rings
and makes our vows priceless, precious things.

BUTTERCUPS AND WHITETHORN

This is the time of year
when my lungs get all romantic
and declare themselves asthmatic.
It's ever-so-slightly tragic.
Keatsian, almost. Sheer

bliss to be alive
when everything's reborn
in buttercups and whitethorn
all of a mid-May morn,
kissing awake my five

senses with the softest
lips I've ever tasted.
Primrose soft. Ingested
with every breath, but wasted
on my consumptive chest.

It's not all woe, however.
I find some consolation
in the fragrance of the season
that stirs my imagination
and makes me more a lover

of fields and birds and sky
than your average individual,
l'homme moyen sensuel,
could ever be; the thrill
of birdsong enters my

bosom like a balm
when I walk through early evening
all lit up with the leaving
of trees and twilight deepening
into a pool of calm

I actually can enter,
like a pilgrim seeking ease
from some spiritual disease
who finds that he can breathe
a sweeter draught of air

when he steps into the garden
of wonder and belief
in miracles, the chief
being May in her mild mid-leaf
of buttercups and whitethorn.

River

It's only a stretch
of the Clanrye
running to Derryleckagh
and on into Newry,

coming from somewhere
up in the Mournes,
away beyond Hilltown,
at the stony horizon's

edge, but it graces
the valley that lies
between Benagh on one side
and Croreagh. On Sundays

I take our dog, Fluffy,
down to the river
and let him chase rabbits
while I watch midges hover

over the shallow
sun-shadowed depths
of the water, just watching
its brightness eclipse

all other worries
and letting time flow
on in its own sweet
time, letting go.

Summer Reading

Sat in my granda's garden reading *Ulysses,*
the siren-song of summer in the air,
I brooded upon love's bitter mysteries,

surrounded by the sounds of birds and bees,
and lost myself in longing thoughts of her,
sat in my granda's garden reading *Ulysses,*

her hair in sunlight, shining like the sea's
surface in the morning, silent, where
I'd brooded upon love's bitter mysteries

and called her name out to the waves, 'Marese',
like Stephen atop a tram in Howth, soul bare,
(sat in my granda's garden reading *Ulysses*)

both of us answered only by the breeze
of indifferent nature, making me aware
I brooded upon love's bitter mysteries

in vain, gazing into the sunstruck darkness
of Joyce, eyes burning with anguish and despair,
sat in my granda's garden reading *Ulysses,*
and brooded upon love's bitter mysteries

Mourne Country

for Tony Keenan and Damien Boyd

Time is slow moving here.
You sense centuries in the air,

like eagle, hawk and falcon, high
and burning in the mist-veiled sky,

every time you're in these mountains.
Millennia, even, a granite silence

surrounding you like open weather,
wind whispering through the heather,

heath grass, harebell, bracken, blackthorn,
reeds, bulrushes, whirlpool, rock cairn

of ancient hero, poet's *spéirbhean*,
rebel, redcoat, Óglaigh na hÉireann,

ghostly shades of long-lost lovers,
covert SAS manoeuvres

above the forests, villages, hill farms,
the seaside town's lachrymose charms

you left behind an hour ago,
risking sunstroke, vertigo,

to follow walls of stone on stone
leading up to pure horizon

where you scan land and sea
and fill your lungs with history.

SUMMER STORM

Halfway through another
week, the sullen silence
of July burst in downpour,
thundercrack, sheet lightning,

every ominous instant
an x-ray of itself,
past, future, present
a swirling tarot pack.

Suddenly, summer's mood
was feverish, electric;
flashing eyes, like jewels, outside
my window, diabolic.

The dark was elemental,
alive. I lay and listened,
lover-like, tensed, in thrall.
The bare horizon glistened

until the whole thing was over.
Then, a rarer silence
blossomed, like a flower.
I felt a breath, a cadence,

and woke again in bed
rediscovering the rain,
its half-intoned, half-muttered
sobs of desolation.

Saturday Night, Sunday Morning, Carlingford

Above the port of Carlingford
the castle of King John stands guard

against the dark. The summer moon
is like a skull or a doubloon

in the sapphire sky. The violet sea
is like a flower, swaying gently,

in the soft night air that carries scents
of seaweed, salt, the iridescence

of stars reflected, the Milky Way
shimmering all across the bay

like a shoal of herring in mid-flight
pursuing its own wild delight

on up the coast to Newcastle.
Back in Carlingford, a dull

languor fills the streets. It's late
and no one troubles the old toll gate

with knocking at this peaceful hour.
The pubs are shut, a mildly sour

smell of stout the only hint
of stag dos, hen nights, transient

'nights to remember', until morning
wakes to seagulls' fierce storm warning

of time and tide, thirst, desire,
sunshine on slate roofs, like fire.

The Blueness of Cheese

It's hardly Havanna
but Dundalk in the summer
during a downpour
descended from nowhere
is my kind of banana-

republican town.
Streets are all drenched,
flower baskets quenched,
storm shutters clenched
as the pink heavens open

on the old Latin quarter,
the piazzo, cathedral,
the Imperial Hotel,
the brewery, the gaol,
boats in the harbour,

fishmonger, florist,
butcher, bookseller,
ladies' hairdresser,
gentleman's outfitter,
vintner, tobacconist,

creating a lush
steam-tropical backdrop,
full of palm trees, the drip-
drop music that hap-
ens in the afternoon hush

of a colonial city
in pre-revolutionary
mode, the quiet era
before Castro, Guevara,
pure possibility

filling the air
like the fragrance of jasmine,
inspiring a person
to dream he's *our man,*
not a vacuum cleaner retailer.

THE RETURN OF A KING

Francis Ledwidge died a British soldier
digging roads on the Western Front in Ypres
in teeming rain, 'blown to bits' by shellfire,
amidst the slime-green stench of high summer,

1917. They took his body,
the bits that they could still identify,
and flung it in the shellhole he'd been killed by
to the keen of a blackbird's lonely threnody

from a dripping thorn bush. That night, back in Navan,
glancing out a window, his best friend
saw him sauntering up the street, as full

of leafy life as the countryside round Slane;
the fields, the flowers, the river and the mound
where the dead kings gathered, awaiting his arrival.

The Fifteenth of August

The second cut of silage of the summer
is off the two big fields that shine like honey
pouring down the valley to the river,
full of its own importance in the sunny
aftermath of an afternoon of showers,
its deep green babble braggadocio
in the peaceful stillness after teatime; flowers
in hedgerows, butterfly and swallow
aerosolling living swathes of colour,
cattle on the far bank looking Buddhist,
mystic calm in the shades of sycamore
and life itself slowed down to the pace
of grass growing, water flowing, grace
a gift, like Mary, immaculate, was promised.

TWO SKETCHES OF A SONGBIRD

I

I didn't know
what kind of bird
it was I heard
outside my window

this morning when
my senses wakened
to its sound
just after dawn

singing August
with such pleasure
and *joie de vivre*
it surely must

have been in love
with all the world
or been a herald,
a holy dove,

sent to announce
an age of grace
had come upon us,
but all at once

I felt the calm
of sunlight, leaves,
fields full of sheaves,
sweet-throated autumn,

and suddenly
not knowing was
the thrilled surprise of rhapsody.

II

But now I learn
my lovely songbird's
a kind of woodkerne-
warrior, dis-

olving through
the sylvan dark
of dawnlight's blue-
grey mizzle-murk,

its song a shield,
a war cry sent
across three fields
with one intent;

to warn his foes
and rivals not
to cross him. Crows
and ravens note

the tempered steel
beneath the silk,
the iron will,
no ounce of milk-

y softness there –
only the fierce,
bloody desire
to rend and pierce,

and keep away
in rueful knowledge
such rhapsody
is pure gleam, edge.

Apple Season

It's here again, the start of apple season.
My favourite time of year. The apple trees
are burgeoning into fruit in our wee garden
across the road, ablaze with birds and bees,

as August ripens into soft September,
sensuous with nuts and berries, sloes,
damsons, rhubarb, blackcurrant, plum and pear,
as beautiful, in their own way, as a rose.

The cows are back to graze the river meadows
and up our own back field a horse and foal
are fetlock-deep in a summer's worth of grass
and sleepy sunshine, radiant and full

of early autumn's incandescent fire.
The air each morning has a sharper bite,
like apple flesh, intense as love, desire
and sharpening my lover's appetite

for this time of the year, its earthly Eden
all the more seductive for its brief
juice-filled moment glistening in the sun
before the fall, the garden filled with grief.

Milk and Apples

Paul Fearon swore by ordinary milk and apples
while the rest of our class aspired to better things
like Mars or Milky Bar, Toblerone, Wagon Wheels.
Angel Delight was the heaven of our imaginings
but only Georgina Sands, or Yvonne Canavan,
would have actually tasted such fabulous success,
or so they told us. Possibly Joan McClean,
but she was beautiful and that gave her airs and graces.

Now, thirty years later, perusing the introduction
to Faber's edition of Edward Thomas' poems
I read his disdain of pineapple, persimmon,
in favour of honest-to-goodness flavours, hymns
to the earth he stood on, a bit like Paul Fearon
biting the core, proclaiming his real *Te Deums*.

Hawthorn

Isaac Newton discovered wonder
sitting under an apple tree.
You could say it hit him like a thunder-
bolt, but you'd be wrong, *mon ami*.

It hit him like a Flower of Kent
falling in his mother's garden
and teaching him the true extent
of Mother Earth's hold on her children.

William Wordsworth had a similar
epiphany one windy day
out walking by the Ullswater.
Or his sister had, it's hard to say.

Anyhow, he *saw a crowd,*
a host of golden daffodils,
and instantly his soul discovered
the dancing joy that nature fills

the human heart with, if we only
allowed ourselves to open up
and let its wonder heal our lonely
egos with its vital sap.

This lesson, likewise, taught itself
to me today, up our back field.
Not looking where I walked, a Delph-
ic oracle, of a sort, revealed

the utter gorgeousness of love
in the shape of a berry-laden branch
of hawthorn hanging just above
my head that led my eyes to launch

their gaze towards the lustrous blaze
of hawthorn all around me. Trees
full-lipped with August's scarlet rays
dazed me with their ecstasies

of light and left me wonderstruck
like some wild-eyed discoverer
in a book, all windswept and Romantic,
surprised by joy, its pure elixir.

A Rowan

is a leafy lighthouse
at the end of summer
gazing across
the quiet acres

of foxglove, thistle,
their purples, golds,
alder, hazel,
their jades and emeralds

where cattle lie
in nettle-incense,
mist on the sea
of afternoons

of thistledown clouds
like galleons adrift
on azure tides,
air currents soft

with buttery light
rich with the buzz
of insects in flight,
their fabulous voyages

unfathomable
as summer is deep,
as the mist-veil
blurring the shape

of oncoming autumn,
like a great barge
approaching the rowan
with its cargo of damage.

GO!

Was it a woodpigeon I saw
*wwwrrroooosh*ing out of the trees,
its wingflurry defying the law
of Newton with consummate ease,

as it bulleted into the twilight
without so much as a nod
like a lover who's late for a date
and can't stop chewing the cud?

I've been there and known that rush
of adrenaline, love or whatever.
We've all had that terrible crush
on a hot chick who won't wait forever

and is probably on her way home
on the last bus, deleting your number
as she curses agreeing to come
out to meet you, remember?

So I didn't take any offence
as I watched our young stud Romeo
all in a flap to impress
his new girlfriend; said, 'Go to her. *Go*!'

Horse Hair

Feeding the horses
with apples I'd picked
from our tree in the garden,

I risked a caress
of their manes and, unpanicked,
they simply stood on

and I felt happiness
like a lost tune half-majicked
from an old violin.

Avalon

A dank September evening, green and chilly.
The river pours itself down its own gullet
like a bottle of beer being glug-glugged greedily
as I walk along its reedy, rushy dull-lit
ale-flow through the fields, all wet with rain,
every blade of grass a glistening
flute glass holding emerald champagne
raised to toast my presence. I am king,
as Kavanagh almost said, of every drip-
ing hedge and bush and branch and watery blossom
floating in the evening air like visions
of some dream-kingdom from an acid trip
taken by Merlin, Jim or Ivan Morrison,
in search of healing, home, dim Avalons.

FROST

Silently, the world will change tonight.
I sense it in the silence, crystal bright,
a strangeness coalescing out of sight
and turning into morning, snowflake-white
as happiness, as innocence, as light,
pure, Platonic, unironic, quite
perfect, plumb, prismatic, *pleine,* just right.

And then I'll know the time is ripe to write,
to forge my conscience in the stellar quiet
of morning newly minted out of sunlight
glistening all around me, snowdrop-white,
and purifying every sense to insight
such as Keats experienced, his 'Bright
Star' a hymn to silence, coldness, night.

Leaving Belfast

It's easier to leave than to be left behind.
– 'Leaving New York', R.E.M.

I've had enough of Belfast's bim bam boom!
I'm heading home to Benagh where there's room
to breathe and be myself, whoever that is.
Like Nicolas Cage, as Ben, in *Leaving Las Vegas*,
I'm tired of listening to the lonely teardrops
of my heart crying, standing late at bus stops,

or falling into oblivion, drunk in bars,
getting into rows with total strangers,
always searching for my lover, Sera,
forgetting she was in another era,
in the days of wine and roses, and Van Morrison
singing down the avenues of rain …

Instead, these days and endless nights, it's more a
William Burroughs kind of scene, our hero
ending up in bed with aliens
who hide their faces under synthetic skins
but can't hide their antennae in the morning
when the sun peers through thin curtains, wisdom
    dawning,

whiskey pale, on what his life's become;
a 'crumbled elegance', hard to come back from.
And all around, in this old lonesome town,
the days just get more lonesome as the wine goes down
and the sun goes down … and the lights go up
on another night of drinking on the 'strip'

of the Ormeau Road: The Errigle, The Pavillion,
The Parador, The Hatfield, The Rose & Crown,
wandering starlit out in search of a taxi,
stood on the Ormeau Bridge, filled with such ennui

and self-disgust the river looks the only answer
to all my problems, graceful as a dancer,

the way it glides beneath me in a dream-
sequence slide and shimmy, all Brylcreem
and nonchalance, a languid Fred Astaire
asking me to join it, or Chet Baker
breathing 'My Funny Valentine', its eddies
a soundtrack to my late night sad epiphanies ...

and morning comes, as morning always does,
on Belfast, grimy, grey and lachrymose
with rain, regret, recrimination, rue,
on some sad street or lonely avenue,
the view out over the city to the sea
hazy in morning mist, like memory,

the skyline seagulled, sacred and profane
with churches, temples, towerblocks, bridges, cranes,
but lyrical still with sunlight in the leaves
and swallows flickering in and out of eaves
and starlings recreating Jackson Pollocks
across the morning sky towards the docks,

reminding me of Woody Allen's New
York, hosannaed by *Rhapsody in Blue*
and shot in black and white, its neon haze
forever captured in the camera's gaze,
romantised out of all proportion;
'... to him New York meant beautiful women

and street-smart guys who seemed to know
all the angles ...' reaching a crescendo
of architecture, fireworks, orchestra,
in the edited perfection of nostalgia

for *la jeunesse* all art is at its heart,
a lying down where all the ladders start

and looking up at all those wondrous stars
from various puddles, boating ponds or gutters
and trying to paint a picture, like Van Gogh,
of starry night whilst crashing on the rocks
of loneliness, despair; hungover, broke,
on Botanic Avenue, almost fit to boke,

or falling on the thorns of life and bleeding
all over the place … so that is why I'm leaving …
Belfast has changed and I just haven't; peace
and time have changed the sensibilities
of the beautiful people. Now, the 'bright young things',
hipsters all, are vaping, sexting, tweeting,

drinking craft beer with bearded reverence,
and leaving me behind in their attempts
to build Jerusalem here, their innocence
matched only by their utter confidence
of succeeding soon, forgetting there's no success
like failure and that failure's no success

at all … or something like that … I forget
the words of songs I used to know by heart,
forget, as well, the dreams I used to have
of Greenwich Village, The Gaslight and the grave
chiming bells of freedom; now these mean streets
from some old wars are the scenes of my defeats:

Fitzroy, Cromwell, Delhi, Curzon, Burma,
Candahar, Agincourt, Palestine, Great Victoria,
night after night, me their grim survivor,
walking through dawn, De Niro in *Taxi Driver*,

alienated, angry, talking to myself
in a hundred mirrors, doubting my mental health,

and all I want is home, far from high-rises
springing up like cocaine-fuelled neuroses
out of the old Belfast of Padraic Fiacc
or Carol Reed, shining, glittering, fake
and phony as the world that Holden Caulfield
turned his back on, left behind for rye fields

and children running careless through them … so
I turn my autumn collar up and go
through September's days in search of sunlight, sea,
the jouissance that has always eluded me,
a ragged sculpture of the ragged wind
that blows us all towards the promised end.

Leaving Speech

What *is* there, really, to say
in the end, after twenty years,
beyond the expected stuff,
amusing anecdotes, tears,

a lifetime edited down
to a file page of uninspired, dull
reminiscences, thanks,
sad jokes about golf, the usual

coma-inducing litany
of meaningless nostalgia
for classrooms in September,
clean jotters, blah, blah, blah ...?

While the SLT grows nervous
about where all this is going;
'What we *don't* need, going forward,
is this nutjob *saying* something!'

At the young staff's table
a past pupil looks at her friend
as if to say with her eyes,
'Is this *ever* going to end?'

And the PE guys are already
drifting towards the bar
and some other people are starting
to finger the keys to their car

in anticipation of leaving
before the madness kicks in
and the hotel manager is wondering,
'Have we stocked enough Gordon's Gin?'

So that what gets said, or unsaid,
is lost in the general buzz
and the speaker sits down, his words
attributed genteel applause

that fades into silence and night
and laughter in shadows, and soon
not even that; just himself
and the future, the O of the moon.

Last Chapter

That last autumn in rainy Belfast
nearly killed me; a falling leaf,
dusk descending at ten to four,
were far too much like Brian Moore
in one of his portraits of lonely grief,
the terrible beauty of the past,

for comfort, far too bittersweet
the sense of failure in each sip
I took of evenings, lamplit, dull,
though also strangely beautiful,
each time I headed for a chip
or to the off licence down the street,

'I am stretched on your grave'
by Sinéad O'Connor taking me back
to first year Queen's, the night I slit
my wrists in a drunken, desperate
escape bid from reality's rack,
a place where demons rant and rave.

I felt like Judith Hearne, a ghost
in my own life, not moving on,
just fading further every day
into that moment, grimly grey,
where I'd just disappear, like one
whose number you once had but lost.

A fallen leaf, dusk, a room
in some old novel, emptied of
its previous tenant, genteel rain,
cancerous sadness, pitiless migraine,
an unsent letter sealed with love,
a window view of gloom. And doom.

About the Author

Francis O'Hare was born in Newry, Co. Down, in 1970. He co-authored a volume of poetry, *Outside the Walls,* with Frank Sewell, published by An Clochan Press, Belfast, in 1997. His first full collection, *Falling into an O,* was published by Lagan Press in 2007. A further pamphlet collection was published by Lagan Press in 2009, entitled *Alphaville.* Lagan published his second collection, *Somewhere Else,* in 2011. In the same year, he also published a collection in America, *Home and Other Elsewheres,* with Evening Street Press, Ohio. He has published poems in various journals in Ireland, the UK and the United States, including *Poetry Ireland Review, Evening Street Review, The Galway Review, The Glasgow Review of Books, A New Ulster, Abridged, Honest Ulsterman, The Burning Bush, The Blue Nib* and *The Yellow Nib.*